1

A Complete Look at Anxiety Disorders

Studies on Chronic Anxiousness

By: James M. Lowrance © 2008

INTRODUCTION

Anxiety conditions are the most common of all emotional disorders and affect millions of people in the U.S. and worldwide. This book is a collection of articles derived from extensively researched information, compiled into one complete resource. Some aspects of Anxiety Disorders, their symptom manifestations and coping methods and treatments are addressed more than once in the chapters however, these often bear-repeating and the coverage in one chapter for an aspect of anxiety will contain details not covered by its counterpart chapter. It is my hope that readers will find this book to be a valuable resource for personal anxiety coping or for that in supporting their loved ones who suffer chronic anxiety.

TABLE OF CONTENTS (8 Chapters):

A Complete Look at Anxiety Disorders

CHAPTER ONE

The True Purpose of Anxiety

Thank you for ordering this e-book on the subject of anxiety disorders. The main focus in the following chapters is to help anxiety sufferers learn not to fear the symptoms of anxiety. This is an aspect of "Cognitive Behavioral Therapy" (CBT) that, in my opinion is the single most effective one in overcoming anxiety disorders. I also discuss the importance of stress-reduction because added stressors can result in "anxiety sensitization".

Anxiety is one of the most common emotions we all experience. Without the anxiety mechanism, we might not have the sudden "presence of mind" and the sudden increased ability to react and jump out of the way of an oncoming truck that is barreling down the street, on a direct path to run over us! This mechanism, called the "fight or flight response", that gives us the extra strength and energy, to fight or run, is designed to protect us and so in situations like these (to use a cliché), "anxiety is our friend".

Anxiety also helps us when we have tasks to perform. People who perform as actors in Broadway plays or have important public speeches to make or a Fireman who has a fire to put out etc..., all depend on the fight or flight response, to enhance their performance and to provide them added inspiration for the task at hand, so again, in cases like these, anxiety is our friend.

Symptoms of Anxiety

Anxiety symptoms generally include the following.

- *apprehension*
- *worry*
- *feelings of fear*
- *rapid heart beat*
- *hyperventilation*
- *excessive sweating*
- *blushing*
- *trembling*
- *increased blood pressure*
- *muscle tension*
- *an urge to escape*

A Complete Look at Anxiety Disorders

These symptoms are included in what are called "anxiety disorders" and are experienced to varying degrees, depending upon which anxiety disorder a person is experiencing. The chapters that follow will help us to identify different types of common anxiety disorders.

CHAPTER TWO

When is Anxiety Considered a Disorder?

Dis-ordered anxiety can cause fears and phobias to develop and to cause ordinary situations to become avoided by the one experiencing it. One example of anxiety that develops into a "disorder" is when a person becomes fearful of social situations and settings. A certain degree of anxiety is normal in social settings because it actually lends toward a respectful attitude and helps us to put our best foot forward when making friends and acquaintances but when shyness becomes a full-blown fear, the anxiety then becomes a disorder.

Another way to look at this is to say that under normal circumstances, anxiety happens in the "order" it is supposed to. Unfortunately in some people, the anxiety "fight or flight response", begins to trigger at the inappropriate times, or in a "disordered" fashion. Anything that can be labeled "disordered", must also have the ability to be in the correct "order", just like something that is colored can become discolored.

The way in which anxiety can become a "disordered" thing, is when it does not happen at the appropriate time or is "out of the order" in which it was meant to be. This does not make the anxiety itself an unnatural thing, only the timing becomes unnatural! Anxiety becomes "Anxiety Disorder", when a person has developed learned behaviors, that causes it to activate more often than it should or due to things that have become triggers for anxiety that normally should not be.

Triggers are also called "phobias", meaning simply "fears" of various different things. Some people develop more fears, due to the anxiety reaction itself. The fight or flight response to specific things can be experienced and perceived as "negative" by a person and they will then have that negative type of response to that same experience/trigger, repeatedly, until they are able to overcome that fear/phobia.

Other persons exposed to those same triggers, might have positive anxiety reactions to them, that we might actually call "positive excitement".

An example of this might be a person who becomes, phobic around snakes and their anxiety response feels very negative to them when seeing a snake and this triggers their phobia. Another person who loves seeing and being around snakes, might instead become curiously excited and have just as powerful an adrenaline surge (fight or flight response), when seeing a snake but instead of it causing them to run away from the snake, it makes them want to chase after it and catch it. This is not such a ridiculous example because I have a nephew, who when he was a child, caught many snakes and other unusual creatures and loved every minute of it, despite being bitten a few times!

The point of this look at the term "disorder", as related to anxiety, is so that we can better understand that anxiety can be used positively or negatively in our lives. No one has anxiety mastered to the point that it works for them positively in every situation they experience but it gives each of us a goal in life, to learn to channel anxiety into positive energy as often as we possibly can. We can also work on those phobias, to try and change them into positive experiences; so that the negative feelings begin to fade (Easier said than done and takes practice).

A Complete Look at Anxiety Disorders

One person can experience an adrenaline surge as a very negative experience, such as someone who has a negative panic reaction to a rollercoaster ride, while another person on the same ride, will have just as strong an adrenaline reaction but will experience it as fun and exciting!

People with Anxiety Disorders should be encouraged to know that with help through treatments, such as "Cognitive Behavioral Therapy" and other positive treatments and therapies they can learn over time, to change those learned behaviors, so that more anxiety reactions, become positive, rather than negative experiences.

CHAPTER THREE

Four Common Anxiety Disorders

Generalized Anxiety Disorder (GAD): This common anxiety disorder manifests with chronic worry as a major symptom. It affects an estimated 6.8 million Americans and affects twice as many adult women as men. People with this anxiety disorder find themselves worrying intensely and continually about everyday issues, such as work, relationships, school and health. While most people worry to a degree about these same issues, people with GAD do so to an exaggerated extent and on an ongoing basis (chronic). The worry aspect of this anxiety disorder also involves unrealistic or irrational worries as well, such as having constant concern over "what might happen", even if the chances are that the things being worried about will not happen. This type of worry over irrational concerns is also sometimes referred to as "what if thinking" and is also a feature of other anxiety disorders. According to some mental health sources, a person must have this type of severe worrying for at least six months for it to be considered as a possibility for being Generalized Anxiety Disorder.

Social Anxiety Disorder (SAD): We all have a degree of apprehension when it comes to meeting new people or attending social events and settings. People with SAD will have an exaggerated fear of socializing, which is also referred to as "social phobia." With this anxiety disorder, shyness becomes extreme and causes the person to begin to avoid social situations and to become extremely anxious when they are required to attend such events or to meet new people, even when it is individuals rather than a group.

People with social anxiety disorder find themselves experiencing heightened anxiety symptoms in social settings, such as feelings of panic, excessive sweating, trembling and hyperventilation (rapid breathing). Much of what brings on these symptoms in people with SAD is the fear of being judged by others who are observing them or of looking silly or stupid in from of them. This phobia, affecting 15 million American adults, causes them to avoid social events and settings.

Panic Disorder (PD): The majority of Americans have had a panic reaction to some type of event at some time in their lives.

But for 6 million American adults, panic reactions or "panic attacks" begin to trigger on a continual basis. This indicates the development of panic disorder. Having an occasional panic attack, does not point to panic disorder, but if a person has a panic attack every day or several a day, this strongly indicates that the disorder has developed. For many people with panic disorder, it was the original panic attack that then causes them to experience more of them. Because the original attack was so unpleasant, the fear (phobia) of having additional panic attacks serves as a trigger for causing them afterward. Panic attacks include all of the symptoms listed previously in chapter one but with panic, the symptoms happen forcefully and suddenly, and create what might be referred to as a "climax" of anxiety.

Post Traumatic Stress Disorder (PTSD): This anxiety disorder results from experiences that are extremely traumatizing to a person. Once the event has taken place, the person is unable to fully recover from it emotionally. The event that triggers PTSD can be an act of violence perpetrated upon them or witnessed by them, a severe accident that causes severe shock or a sudden loss of a loved one. The person with PTSD will often relive the traumatic event by having it replay repeatedly in their mind.

This replay may not be voluntary, but simply a deeply embedded memory they cannot shake from their subconscious. A PTSD sufferer will also sometimes experience nightmares relating to the traumatic event or possibly even experience flashbacks that cause them to believe they are actually reliving the event repeatedly. War veterans, who are traumatized while fighting in combat duty, will commonly experience this anxiety disorder. An estimated 7.7 million Americans suffer from PTSD.

CHAPTER FOUR

Anxiety Sensitization

There, is a phase that most anxiety suffers are very familiar with having experienced, as part of their anxiety condition, called; "Anxiety Sensitization". This is a state of sensitivity an anxiety sufferer can reach, when they have experienced an extra amount of stress, over a period of time and it causes them to reach a heightened state of being sensitive to anxiety feelings. When a person reaches this stage of heightened sensitivity to anxiety, they will experience anxiety reactions more easily. Anxiety responses to things will also be more easily triggered while in this state.

An anxiety sufferer, who reaches this state of sensitivity, may become concerned that they have entered a more severe stage of anxiety disorder however, these phases are almost certain to be temporary increases in the anxiety condition and not a permanent worsening of the condition.

Once they can achieve relief from their added stressors; they will often see the sensitivity diminish.

When a person is extra tired or extra stressed, they have less resistance to any negative feelings and medical research states that there is also less resistance to physical illnesses when one is stressed-out. Most anxiety sufferers can likely also relate to the fact, that when you are physically weak from an illness or feeling extra tired, this can also cause anxiety to be triggered more easily because one is in a less resistant state.

People with anxiety conditions, should observe those times when they reach this state of becoming sensitized to anxiety, so that they can learn to reverse some of the trends that lend toward getting stressed out. For example; if staying involved in mental studies, such as being on the computer for too long or doing paper work, such as tax returns, for extended periods, results in feeling stressed out and sensitized to anxiety, a person needs to learn to pace their self, instead of taking on too much of these type activities at a time. It is also a good idea not to take on too many duties at once (multi-tasking), in trying to get them all accomplished too quickly. This too is a stress-producer and one should instead be looking for stress-reducers.

Some ideas for stress-reducing, in addition to the things mentioned above, would be to take time out to do things that are enjoyable and pleasurable. If one enjoys being outdoors to observe all of the natural beauty and fresh air, then they should take time out of their duties and take a nature walk or just sit under a shade tree, with a glass of decaffeinated tea and relax. If exercise is a stress reducer for a person (and it is for many people), then leave they should leave their duties behind for a while and get some exercise. This should be done as often as needed to keep stress levels down, as long as one does not exceed their tolerance for exercise. Persons with Generalized Anxiety Disorder, tend to be the type of anxiety sufferers, who push themselves too hard and try to get too many things done in unreasonably short periods of time. This is often due to their worries about things getting piled up on them, if they don't stay ahead of their duties. Gad sufferers also stay busy, because it helps them experience some relief from their constant worry and free-floating anxiety feelings. This trend however, can also end in periods of feeling stressed out, so that there is a vicious cycle of seeking stress relief that instead actually results in causing excessive stress.

People with Gad and other anxiety conditions, should work on these methods for reducing stress but should also not become overly concerned if they should reach one of these stressed out phases, that causes them to be sensitized to anxiety. The phase will pass and afterward, another opportunity will present itself, to again work on eliminating the trends that lead to these phases.

It is also important for anxiety sufferers to remember that if they do reach the point of anxiety sensitization, it will not cause them insanity, or death from intense, ongoing periods of anxiety. Adrenaline, the major anxiety producing hormone, can only reach a certain level and then can go no further. The human body is designed, so that it will only utilize a certain amount of adrenaline at a time because it can only metabolize that amount, at any given time. The sensations from being overly-adrenalized are unpleasant but they will pass, given time.

It is important to work on stress-reducing techniques, incorporating exercise, deep-breathing techniques (slow diaphramic breathing, inflating the stomach rather than the chest) and any other methods that one knows will help them to avoid or reduce those stressed out phases.

A Complete Look at Anxiety Disorders

19

Not reducing stress or avoiding it when possible, can lead to becoming sensitized to anxiety. With time, practicing good stress-reduction methods, can help one to overcome and conquer negative anxiety experiences in their life.

CHAPTER FIVE

Catastrophic Thinking

A young lady recently e-mailed me after reading one of my online articles on an anxiety subject, asking if having bizarre thoughts about terrible things was common with severe anxiety states. I assured her that these type thoughts were indeed common to anxiety sufferers and that the name for them is "catastrophic thinking".

She had described to me, that when severe anxiety states occurred with her, she would have racing thoughts, many of them having to do with the fear of losing control and hurting herself, or others and sometimes the thought included that of even harming her own baby. This was understandably very concerning to her because like many anxiety sufferers, she believed these violent, sadistic and tragic type thoughts, indicated that she was on the verge of losing her sanity.

The fact is however, that catastrophic thinking, happens commonly with anxiety sufferers and many people refer to it as "what if thinking".

Anxiety Disorder patients describe thoughts like the above ones, that the young lady described but these can also include other fearful thoughts, such as thinking one will lose control in front of other people and make a complete fool of their self. Other anxiety patients may have thoughts of passing out and needing an ambulance, but not being in a location where others will notice and call for help. Others describe thoughts of snapping and becoming violent to others around them or of running down a supermarket isle, screaming at the top of their lungs.

One of the reasons catastrophic thinking is so unpleasant, other than for the reasons already stated, is because these thoughts will increase and intensify already present anxiety conditions. Catastrophic thinking in fact, can be a trigger for panic attacks. These "what if thoughts", tend to lead from one to another, until multiple fearful thoughts, are all happening at once, which could be refer to as the "snowball effect". The thoughts gain momentum and loom larger and scarier to the sufferer, as they increase during anxiety states.

Why are these catastrophic type thoughts so common to anxiety sufferers?

According to anxiety researchers, they believe, these thoughts happen because the "fight or flight response", will trigger a mechanism, having to do with our thought processes, which begins to scan for possible dangers. Of course with anxiety disorders, there are no real dangers that are eminent and so the mind will tend to consider possibilities for why the body is reacting as it is, by triggering the fight or flight response. This scanning for dangers, is actually part of the protection mechanism, meant to keep us safe however, the person experiencing them, will misinterpret this as meaning they will actually act on these thoughts and fulfill them.

Let me assure you that this is not the case with anxiety-induced catastrophic thoughts. The fact that the thoughts are scary to you in itself, is proof that you do not wish to act on them. Someone who is actually considering such actions will actually take pleasure in these type thoughts when contemplating them, rather than fearing them and resisting them. These type thoughts are very common to anxiety disorder sufferers and do not in any way, indicate that one is losing their sanity or actually about to snap and go out of control.

The best way to overcome the fear of such thoughts which will in turn also cause them to fade away and stop happening is to reassure one's self of these facts. I have read the testimonials of anxiety sufferers who actually learned to see humor in these thoughts, rather than being terrified of them and this resulted in catastrophic thinking, losing its power in their lives. This is of course easier said than done but with time and repeated reassuring of one's self it can be accomplished, with very good results.

When you think about it, these type thoughts can actually be humorous and one might even add a little humor to them, as they begin happening! For example, if one has a fear of losing control, they can add to that thought, the idea of climbing a tree and hanging from a limb, upside down by their legs. This might sound like a ridiculous method but it can be as effective as any other method, in diverting these type thoughts and getting them more under control.

A final bit of advice I would give however, is not to make it a fight or struggle, any more than one has to, instead, they should almost make a little game out of it, or see it as an interesting experiment because anxiety seems to thrive on struggle.

Once one gains ground on catastrophic thinking, they will see the struggle aspect of gaining control of their thoughts, fade away and over time, it will automatically be replaced with pleasant, positive thoughts and thinking.

CHAPTER SIX

Depersonalization and Derealization

There is a common symptom-phenomenon anxiety disorder sufferers will experience, called "depersonalization and de-realization". These occur commonly in patients with anxiety disorder and sometimes also in those with clinical depression, who suffer experience co-existing anxiety and can be very concerning to them. What I wish to do in this chapter is to explain what these symptoms are and to offer some comfort to those who may suffer Anxiety Disorder by relating the fact that both of these categories of unreality symptoms are experienced commonly with these emotional disorders and in the vast majority of the time, they are neither harmful nor dangerous.

Depersonalization

This symptom phenomenon commonly found in anxiety disorder sufferers, but especially those with panic attacks, is a symptom-induced experience, in which a patient feels as if they are "unreal", like they no longer exist as a person. They may even feel they have become invisible and that others around them are real but they are not.

A Complete Look at Anxiety Disorders

Some patients describe it as feeling like being a robot and no longer like a human being. Patients have described episodes for example, of looking at their own hand, in front of their face and wondering if it is really there. Patients will also describe experiences of looking into a mirror and actually feeling as if they do not recognize themselves and they feel as if they are possibly having some type of identity crisis. Obviously, these are very scary and very unpleasant experiences for anxiety patients and ones they certainly do not want to continue or to reoccur.

These episodes of depersonalization are reported by some anxiety disorder sufferers, to happen immediately preceding the onset of a panic attack or with other severe anxiety symptoms, while others experience depersonalization during an attack of severe anxiety or panic symptoms. Once the depersonalization symptom is experienced by some anxiety suffers, they report that it will occur more frequently and will be triggered more easily afterward, even with less severe anxiety symptoms.

Derealization

This aspect of unreality symptoms is similar but in this case, that which seems to become unreal is the person's surroundings.

With de-realization, an anxiety sufferer will have episodes of experiencing feelings that their surroundings have become unreal. They will feel as if even reality itself is no longer something they can fully grasp, during those moments but this simply a sensation and they are not actually losing touch with reality. They may even question the existence of things and wonder if life itself is a dream of some type. Some descriptions I have heard of this experience are described as feeling like "being inside of a bubble", or "like trying to see everything, through a curtain" and "like everything is covered with a thick fog".

Many anxiety sufferers will experience both depersonalization and de-realization, at the same time or these may alternate, so that they experience each one at different times. During episodes of either, they will also commonly experience mind fog, meaning they feel hazy and unable to concentrate. These features only add to the unpleasantness of these experiences.

What causes these strange feelings of depersonalization and de-realization that are so concerning to anxiety sufferers?

Well we know the "fight or flight response" itself is a protection mechanism, created in us, to help us flee or flight danger and to help us perform more powerfully, when important tasks are at hand. These unreality type symptoms, in which things seem to become unreal is very likely part of that same protection mechanism. It may be that our minds will cause ourselves and our surroundings, to temporarily fade from our minds and into the background, in order for us to concentrate more intensely, on locating any actual danger that threatens us, whether real or imagined. It is similar to the reason an anxiety patient's mind will race at times, because it is trying to scan for dangers that have threatened them and that are setting off the fight or flight response. We also know that physical senses are heightened during strong anxiety responses and this too likely adds to these feelings of unreality.

What is important for anxiety sufferers to know and to understand is the fact that these unreality symptoms do not indicate the onset of insanity or of one losing their mind. They are very common occurrences with anxiety conditions and will not cause damage to a person's mind or sanity.

The fear of going crazy is a very concerning one to those who experience severe anxiety episodes and also to those with clinical depression and these two often co-exist but these are irrational thoughts and will not take place.

True Psychosis

Psychosis is the term for one actually losing touch with reality and having delusions and hallucinations. It is the term for actual mental disorders that may or may not have significant emotional aspects to them. Anxiety and common clinical depression are both in the neurosis category, meaning they are stress related and not caused by an underlying mental disorder. Persons with severe forms of depression, such as Bipolar Disorder, may have psychotic episodes but the more common type depression, called Clinical or Major Depression, is not in the psychosis category. Estimates by some Mental Health Organizations state that psychosis affects an estimated 1% of the U.S. population, whereas the more common anxiety and depression conditions, affect a much higher percent of the population (some place the statistic exceeding 40%).

Patients with severe anxiety conditions need to learn not to fear these unreality type symptoms because adding more fear will intensify and extend the duration of these episodes. This is of course more easily said than done but with time and effort, those with Anxiety Disorders can learn to have less fear of these unreality symptoms, so that the symptoms are what fade into the background rather than the realities of self and surroundings.

If you are an anxiety and/or depression sufferer and are concerned by these unreality type symptoms, I recommend conducting a search on the internet, using the search term "Anxiety De-realization and Depersonalization" and you will find many resource articles stating facts in regard to how common these unreality symptoms are and the fact that they are not harmful or dangerous. In fact another search, using another search term; "Anxiety Depersonalization and De-realization, neither harmful nor dangerous" will yield even more articles that will help in this area. These unreality symptoms are very commonly experienced and not dangerous, although extremely unpleasant.

CHAPTER SEVEN

Calming Yourself during Panic Attacks or Severe Anxiety Episodes

A panic attack is a climax of anxiety symptoms that causes them to be experienced suddenly and forcefully. The symptoms may include the following.

• intense fear
• rapid heart rate
• hyperventilation
• an urge to escape
• muscle tension
• dizziness
• sweating
• mild to moderate pain and pressure in the chest

People, who experience frequent panic attacks, have a condition referred to as Panic Disorder". The following four steps which are often used in different variations of Cognitive Behavioral Therapy techniques (CBT) can help those who suffer panic attacks, to calm their selves when experiencing them.

A Complete Look at Anxiety Disorders

***Remind yourself during a panic attack, that you will
not drop dead or lose your sanity.***

While panic attacks are the most unpleasant type of
anxiety that can be experienced, reputable mental
health sources state that they do not lead to loss of
sanity, strokes or heart attacks, in otherwise healthy
people. Anxiety is a normal mechanism, designed to
give the body increased strength to escape danger or
to fight an enemy should situations arise requiring
the need to do so. It is also designed to help us
accomplish urgent or important duties that life might
present to us. Panic attacks are an example of this
important mechanism, occurring "out of context"
meaning they are triggered at times when there is no
actual need for the "fight or flight" response.

While this improper timing makes panic attacks
extremely unpleasant, they are still a normal
response the body is designed to experience without
causing injury to the mind or body. The real damage
chronic anxiety conditions result-in is restricting
some of the freedom and enjoyments of life rather
than actually causing mental or physical damage.
Reminding yourself of these simple facts, can help
diminish the effects of a panic attack and lend
toward calming yourself down during one.

A Complete Look at Anxiety Disorders

Focus on the task you are involved in rather than focusing on the panic attack symptoms.

While this step is certainly easier said than done, with practice, you can learn to divert your attention away from the unpleasant anxiety symptoms and direct your focus more on accomplishing an immediate goal at hand. The triggers that cause a panic attacks can be simple things such as waiting in line to be checked out at a grocery store or walking to the front isle of a theater to be seated. Other times things that cause panic attacks are of more importance and significance, such as standing before an audience to make an important speech or rescuing someone from a burning home. Regardless of the tasks needing performed, you can practice focusing more on accomplishing them than on the panic symptoms they may be triggering. This will channel your attention toward your energy in performing these tasks, rather than upon surviving the anxiety symptoms that are attempting to challenge you.

If you feel panic symptoms arising while being checked out at the grocery line, you might consider focusing intently on the magazines or other items near the checkout stand.

A Complete Look at Anxiety Disorders

When your groceries are being checked out, you might consider mentally calculating the total cost of your groceries to see how close you come to the final tally. If it helps to join in with the clerk in bagging the groceries, you might consider this as a diversion from focusing on anxiety symptoms. Any method that helps you divert your attention and energy into a task rather than focusing on the anxiety is acceptable and you can also make a game out of it, so that you look forward to the gains you will make over time and actually begin to enjoy accomplishing these goals.

Realize that you are not alone in experiencing panic attacks and that they are not a sign of weakness.

Panic attacks are experienced by an estimated 6 million Americans or about 1 out of every 75. Mental health professionals who study anxiety disorders, including panic attacks, have found that people who suffer chronic anxiety, are many times the more creative and passionate people in our society. Famous sports figures including pro football players Earl Campbell and Ricky Williams have suffered panic attacks, as well as famous celebrities including Howie Mandel and Oprah Winfrey.

A Complete Look at Anxiety Disorders

This places people who suffer panic attacks and panic disorder in good company with some of our nation's most ambitious people. By reminding yourself that greatly admired and creative people suffer chronic anxiety conditions, you can also view yourself as among the most creative and passionate people of our society.

Channel your anxiety into a positive and creative process.

Many anxiety sufferers have found that when they feel on edge or as if they are on the verge of experiencing a panic attack, they are also at their most creative and passionate level. By taking that anxiety energy and channeling it into positive actions, you can redirect it away from negative experiences. Rather than running from the anxiety symptoms or attempting to escape from them when they occur, try channeling that energy into creating something you enjoy. If you enjoy sculpting, writing or painting, allow the anxiety to trigger your creative juices into flowing by concentrating that energy into those creative arts. If you enjoy sports, such as soccer, tennis or martial arts, channel that anxiety energy into improving upon your skills and techniques in these areas.

If you are involved in something or in a location where this is not possible to actually practice these pastimes when anxiety symptoms occur, you might attempt to mentally play the sport in your mind or carry a small notepad for jotting down notes on how you can improve in the sport when you are able to play again.

While the following final-suggestion for this step might seem unusual, there is a UK website that recently reported that a PhD Stress Management Expert in the U.S. found that anxiety and stress relief can be experienced using romantic and sexual fantasy as an anxiety diversion technique.

In his research, he found that people who conjure torrid fantasies involving romantic and sexual scenarios have found that it helps them to divert negative anxiety responses into passionate imagination, with positive results.

I would also add the suggestion that you use your spouse and life partner as the object of your fantasies, which will improve both your anxiety symptoms and your love life at the same time.

These are examples of things that can help to diminish the effects of anxiety symptoms. It can also help those who suffer panic attacks, to redirect their anxiety into a positive rather than into a negative direction and outcome.

CHAPTER EIGHT

Is Anxiety Dangerous to Your Health?

Anxiety of itself is never a direct "cause" of strokes or heart attacks but if you are predisposed to having a stroke due to already present health problems such as severe hypertension, it can be a contributing factor or trigger for these. I state this fact which comes from much research I've read by PhD MDs and Psychiatrists over the past several years.

The anxiety "flight or flight" response temporarily elevates bodily functions; heart rate, blood pressure, respiration and sweating, the same way exercise does, which can also be potentially dangerous for people with already existing health-risks but does not pose a danger to otherwise healthy people.

Anxiety itself is a natural emotion and is designed to be triggered often if needed without physically harmful effects. Anxiety is not stress but a "bodily reaction to stress"; a pressure valve in a sense or the body's way of dealing-with and utilizing stress.

A Complete Look at Anxiety Disorders

The hormone - adrenaline/epinephrine that occurs naturally in the body has a limited effect or a cut off level of strength as mentioned previously and is counteracted by the hormone noradrenaline-norepinephrine (the calming hormone). It is metabolized by the body in such a way, that it cannot continue to escalate to extremely high levels and cause death or severe health effects, in otherwise healthy people.

If it could, people would be dropping dead from anxiety left and right every day because statistics state that up to 25% (1 in 4) people have an anxiety problem/disorder at some point in their lives and for a large percent of these people, it is chronic. If anxiety frequently caused severe health problems, we could then say that God or nature has made an error in giving us this protection mechanism.

My purpose in pointing this out is to differentiate from the idea that anxiety "causes" rather than in some cases "contributes" to severe health problems. Anxiety among many other things, can contribute to all kinds of health problems but in most of these conditions, it is not a direct cause of them.

A Complete Look at Anxiety Disorders

One aspect of anxiety is "worry" however, since everyone on earth with very few exceptions, has worry, it has to be severe and chronic (ongoing) to be classified as an anxiety disorder. This type of chronic anxiety can contribute to a variety of health problems as well (i.e. stomach disorders, hives, headaches, etc...) because chronic worry increases bodily functions, but more subtly than do panic reactions.

While some people may believe confusing these terminologies (a "cause" as opposed to a "contributing factor") is not that important, it really is because in some cases it results in wrong diagnoses of proposed causes for health problems, etc... It probably sounds like "semantics" or "playing with words" but it's really not and in my opinion people should know the difference.

Increased adrenaline over long periods of time, does contribute to serious health problems, such as hypertension and high cholesterol that can then directly cause heart problems and stroke, so these latter mentioned health problems (i.e. hypertension and elevated cholesterol) are the direct causes, while anxiety can be a contributing factor but in most cases not a direct cause.

A Complete Look at Anxiety Disorders

Anxiety doesn't cause these problems in all people some anxiety sufferers don't develop hypertension or high cholesterol from prolonged anxiety.

Like everyone else, anxiety sufferers need to incorporate daily exercise into their routine and improved diet practices because this alone can offset any harmful effects from prolonged anxiety which can contribute to hypertension and elevated cholesterol as mentioned above.

It is important in my opinion, for people with anxiety disorders, especially those who experience panic attacks, to know that the harmful effects of anxiety are almost never immediate unless as stated above, there are co-existing, serious health problems also present. By believing anxiety -- a natural emotion, is so very harmful in otherwise healthy individuals, it makes it very difficult for these patients to learn not to fear any immediate effects from anxiety. Learning not fear anxiety symptoms is a major feature of Cognitive Behavioral Therapy (CBT) but is an aspect patients will have little benefit from if they are told that anxiety will directly cause them, strokes, heart attacks or sudden death.

A Complete Look at Anxiety Disorders

All anxiety disorders are treatable through various different therapies, including methods of Cognitive Behavioral Therapy that have been discussed in the preceding chapters. Anti-anxiety and anti-depressant medications can also help to alleviate and diminish anxiety symptoms when these are needed.

These drugs can also be combined with psychiatric therapies such as CBT and other therapies, for added benefit and in some cases may only be needed temporarily.

Types of anti-anxiety medications (benzodiazepines) include the following:

• alprazolam (Xanax®)
• clonazepam (Klonipin®)
• lorazepam (Ativan®)
• diazepam (Valium®)

• buspirone (Buspar®) (this one is a azaspirodecanedione class drug)

Types of anti-depressants (selective serotonin reuptake inhibitors) that also work as anti-anxiety medications include the following:

- paroxetine (Paxil®)
- venlafexine (Effexor®)
- fluoxetine (Prozac®)
- setraline (Zoloft®)
- fluvoxamine (Luvox ®)

If you suspect that you might have a chronic anxiety condition, see your doctor for further evaluation and referral to proper treatments.

(END)